Praise for *Another Word For Love*

"In *Another Word for Love*, Sarah Stern searches for meaning in a broken world. She delights in things around her, whether the El in New York or trees in New Hampshire, finding in them keys to her inner life. I read this book in the light of her clarity, exactitude, and fine intelligence."

—**Grace Schulman**
author of *Without A Claim*

"Vivid and opaque, innocent and sophisticated, Sarah Stern's poems in *Another Word for Love* are so full of life, never more than when they hint at death, that they refuse to sit still on the page. It's us she's catching in these glimmering nets."

—**Karen Durbin**, *Elle*

"Sarah Stern is a poet to watch and relish."

—*Jewish Book World*

But Today Is Different

But Today Is Different

Sarah Stern

RESOURCE *Publications* · Eugene, Oregon

BUT TODAY IS DIFFERENT

Copyright © 2014 Sarah Stern. All rights reserved. Except for brief quotations in critical publications or reviews, no part of this book may be reproduced in any manner without prior written permission from the publisher. Write: Permissions. Wipf and Stock Publishers, 199 W. 8th Ave., Suite 3, Eugene, OR 97401.

Resource Publications
An Imprint of Wipf and Stock Publishers
199 W. 8th Ave., Suite 3
Eugene, OR 97401

www.wipfandstock.com

ISBN 13: 978-1-62564-917-1

Manufactured in the U.S.A.   10/15/2014

In memory of my mother
Helen Gribetz

Contents

Acknowledgments | ix

Part I

Electricity | 3
Lipstick | 4
The Head of a Woman | 6
Trajectory | 8
Upon Seeing an Old Boyfriend on Facebook | 9
Tongue/Fire/Eclipse/Groove | 10
Love Dots | 12
On Hearing Sex in the Neighboring Hotel Room | 14
Elephant Skin | 15
Love me for an hour this afternoon | 16

Part II

The Pacemaker | 19
Red | 21
The World's Fair | 22
The Week of Missing Things and Prayers | 23
Straw | 24
Pelicans | 25
Almost a Year Later | 26
After the Stroke | 27
I Find My Mother Here | 29
Hanukkah Haiku for My Dad | 30
Parts Suspended | 31
Two Weeks Before | 32
Storm King after Shiva | 33
For My Parents | 35
Yizkor | 36

Part III

The Mannequin at Grand Central Station | 39
Turn Back the Clocks | 41
Decorated Generals | 42
CV: On Looking for a Job | 43
For a Woman Veteran | 46
Making Do | 47

Part IV

The Last Two | 51
Summer Suits | 52
Riding Through Van Cortlandt Park in March | 53
For Dora | 54
Old Faithful | 55
Big Families | 56
Leaving the Garden | 57
Jasper Summer | 58
Into the Moonlight | 59
August | 60

Part V

Here | 63
The Fish | 65
Graffiti | 66
The Violin | 67
On This Mountain | 68
Two Lives | 69
Big Basket of Want | 70
Baruch Habah | 71
Prayer | 72

Notes | 73

Acknowledgments

The author gratefully acknowledges the following publications in which these poems first appeared and/or were cited as finalists for various contests.

The American Dream Anthology (finalist): "Red"

FreeFall (short-listed): "On Hearing Sex in the Neighboring Hotel Room" and "After the Stroke"

The Man Who Ate His Book: The Best of ducts.org, Volume II (appeared originally in Issue 25): "The Mannequin at Grand Central Station"

Fish Poetry Prize (short-listed): "Tongue/Fire/Eclipse/Groove"

With immeasurable love and gratitude to my husband, Michael, and children, Willie and Zoe. With love to my brothers and other family and friends who have encouraged me all these years. With much appreciation and great affection for the One O'Clockers: Guillermo Castro, Maura Candela, John Couturier (additional appreciation for John's hours of proofreading and editing), Shira Dentz, Ron Drummond, Katie Johntz, Amy Lemmon, Katrinka Moore, Martie Palar, Joan Lauri Poole, and Elizabeth Poreba; and to the Bronx best: Amy Gottlieb, Greg McDonald, Anthony Purdy, Samina Shahidi, and Sam Turner. With much fondness for all my wonderful EastWest Institute colleagues, especially for Andrew Nagorski, Alex Schulman, Dragan Stojanovski, and Sarah Miles Williams. With many thanks to David Korzenik for his wise counsel. With much appreciation for Wipf and Stock Publishers, especially for Matthew Wimer.

With special thanks to Edward Hirsch, Cynthia Zarin, Grace Schulman, Karen Durbin, and the Bronx Council on the Arts.

Part I

Electricity

In the back of the small cab in India
our knees touched.
I wanted to ask you,
Do you feel it? And you'd say what?

I'd answer—that attraction—
that spark that my mother
warned me about, *Don't ever pull
out a plug from the wall with wet hands.*

But I did it anyway,
and there it was
a flash and then a zap
right through me. I lived.

And here we live too—
the beautiful children
peer in on us,
the man with 1½ arms

bangs on our window. I'm sorry.
I'm sorry that I can't make
this world right.
He looks back at me and moves on

as I feel the electricity again
in Old Delhi, the chickens
in cages squawking, heaps of orange flowers.
The black goat with blue eyes

in the car next to us
takes it all in, even those knees next to mine
and my groin, how peculiar and selfish
we are with our desires.

Lipstick

Tell me once and for all
that I'm beautiful—
that's what I heard her say
as she looked in the mirror
at the Union Square location
at lunch time.

    We are all art
    of some form but we don't last.
    That's the thing, ephemeral, mortal,
    wonderful English-major words
    that we don't use enough.
    I want to use them in sentences as often as possible.

The lipstick mark on my coffee cup
reminds me that I am a woman.
It took more than 40 years for that realization,
that declaration. I like it.
It's called Saturday from Sephora.
How the women test and retest

    facing the mirrors,
    shadows, liners, mascara, blushes—
    azure rain
    blue dawn
    trio for hazels
    cupid
    wild indigo
    think bronze
    black night.

The idea of womanhood
forever in transition,
my periods getting closer together now
as with pregnancy, no two women
are the same,
they'll never be.

My friend said that sex now
is more difficult because everything
is all papery down there.
The walls are thinning—
mine haven't thinned yet, but I'm sure
I'm not far behind.

And the walls—the oldest art
ever found in the caves
with Werner Herzog narration.
Yes, I want a movie about what happens
to us in all of our glory,
for it is glorious.

The Head of a Woman

After Obama's second inauguration
I went to the Guggenheim.
I wanted to praise
God that no one was shot
and what better place to do that
than here, where She rests,
where She goes to have a beer with
the better angels of our nature

                              where parents bring their
                               children for exposure,
                    the kids point and grin at breasts
            and pubic hair—I hear a mother say—*yes, that's her vagina,*
                      where the Orthodox go on dates
                in public so they won't touch each other
                          even in front of *The Lovers,*
                 where the rest of New York City goes
                        to remember why we live here,
             for the pleasure of knowing this is near.

So tell me dear God, tell me something.
You're grand in the space of an afternoon
with the winter gold about you
everybody seems to be staring up,
your nakedness a strange beacon.

                                After, following the reservoir
                I see the south skyline come into itself,
                 the groggy giants peering into the park,
                          satiated like the turtles
                          that were mating here
                      last spring along the edge,
                        several pairs in reeds,
                          a tourist was filming
                   an afternoon of lovemaking.

Like Picasso. He made love to his muses.
Could I make love to mine?
Last night I did,
but today is different.

                        As I leave the park and head west
                toward Broadway I think of the book
                  I just finished, the beautiful lines
                    that I'll never come across again
             for the first time, but it won't matter
                  because I will have changed

as She did when I turned away
and looked back up
the museum's spiral—
an opening revealed itself—the children
wondered what had happened
all of us, still.

Trajectory

I see it in the morning on occasion
a used condom
on the street.
I want to know
the backstory.
Was it casual sex?
I'm hoping it was so good for both.
Or an affair that's finally official?
Teenagers in love?
A paid transaction?
A rekindling of something
in the back of an old Pontiac?
It's spring and I'm thinking rebirth,
lambs, hay.
It looks sad and lonely,
splayed out on concrete.
What is it about our trajectories—
the arc of our lives
the Bolero in all of us.
I can't accept that all's been done.
It hasn't.
We could do it
with the shades up, the neighbors across the way
and the sparrows banging inside the air conditioner.
We could reinvent ourselves endlessly.

Upon Seeing an Old Boyfriend on Facebook

What was it that ended it more than 20 years ago?
You didn't want to make the commitment.

You wanted to keep dating.
I wanted us to be either all or nothing.

So how come when I see your picture now
it makes me happy—happy?

Strange—I have no hard feelings.
How wild in love I was with you.

I'm smiling now. A flash of me at 21
comes roaring through.

You broke my heart,
and what a heart it was.

Tongue/Fire/Eclipse/Groove

*

I want to make love
to you my breasts against yours
my tongue in you hard.

I want you to come
so that I hear it loud
in my mouth gone mad.

Tell me how this goes
This shift first snow today snow
White stars burning.

**

Dark horse stands in the corral
White fence, frozen earth.

    She is circling and staring off in the distance
    Her mane soft coal.

You've entered me like fire
I'm black and blue waiting for you.

***

    I knew then at 3 a.m.
    Out on the terrace 23 degrees
    I shouted it at the moon
    Copper/yellow/egg
    An iota of nothingness in my winter coat
    And my son's basketball sneakers,
    I looked up, the stars shining
    With a light that pierced/changed me
    My voice echoed over the park and Henry Hudson
    I was standing in the night air
    Shouting for all time
    I love you to no one—to you.

****

Why does food taste so good
when I'm with you

I keep everything from when
we're together—even the stubs—

as though they were the hours
we were together

I don't erase your message
Your voice for the listening

Caught wave
Tell me when this will end

Or is this what it will be
You and me

Sick with aching sweet
Nothing a kind of smooth want

You are the water
I the stone

You're beginning to leave
A contour, a groove

On me
Feel it.

Love Dots

I told her that the love thing has to stop.

What do you mean by the love thing?

You know the crushes, the absurd ones.

Oh, you mean the love dots.

What's a love dot?

It's when a piece of you gets stuck on someone, and you have no control.

Isn't that supposed to happen to teenagers and then you grow out of it?

No, you never grow out of it.

But what do you do?

The question is what does it do to you?

It makes me crazy.

Yes, it does do that, but it makes you see things.

Yes, the colors and shapes.

What else?

I want to shut it down.

Don't.

Why?

Because it changes you, makes you remember that you're more than flesh and bone.

Yes, flesh and bone and trouble.

Can you love it without having it?

Why does it become more beautiful that way?

*It's the stars, the hereafter, the line you heard in the movie—
no promises were made and therefore none were broken.*

On Hearing Sex in the Neighboring Hotel Room

At first it sounded like kids
        banging on the wall,
                laughing, then it was unmistakable.

I wanted to listen and leave at the same time.
        I shouldn't hear this.
                I should hear this.

Was it a couple?
        A whore?
                Just a porn show?

Here's what I wanted to believe:
        It was a couple—they found each other
                all these years later.

The one whose moans I heard
        was coming like she did when she was 23,
                falling into something—

he was remembering her
        as she is, her breasts soft,
                still exquisitely sensitive to his tongue.

His chest still had that
        map-like visual to it—
                Rome squarely between his nipples.

When all was done
        they drank from the same cup,
                looked out at the planes

landing on the runway,
        their lives appearing blurry and uneven
                but somehow meaningful.

It wouldn't happen again, but there was an almost
        religious satisfaction in knowing that the other
                was still humming along, and that was enough.

Elephant Skin

She tells me more than once
to watch the light.
See, she says, look how,

how it dances on the bark,
elephant skin.
I push my body against it—

how this European Copper Beech
welcomes what the day brings
its limbs open and stark

like sex last evening
rolling up to my mouth
those concentric circles of coming

the rings that begin at the root
and work through me
as though I could count them

to know my age.
What is it about this life
that makes it more wondrous

than the day before even with the savagery?
She says, again, praise the light.
So I do, I put my tongue to the beech

in February, you crazy loon you.
No one on the hill except a woodpecker
tap tap tap her little red cap.

Mother used to tell me to know your birds and trees.
I want to know my heart.
Tell me beech what lurks there.

Love me for an hour this afternoon

Love me for an hour this afternoon
Then let's forget what happened
As the light shifts down the avenues

And the offices empty
Watch how the tops of things
Make dreamy collages

The hour and glass, the view
An imprint, a beauty mark
We won't remember anything.

Part II

The Pacemaker

The doctor says that half my mother's heart is closed.
She needs a pacemaker.
She refuses one.
I tell her I love her.
She says she had a good life,
that she loved her husband.
I ask her what she ate today.
Yogurt.
The sweet kind?
Yes.
What else did you do today?
I made a salad.
She wanted her lips
moistened with seltzer.
I asked her if she wanted to
take an anti-depressant.
No, I want to be myself.
But she added that she liked
her sleeping pill.
At 13, I remember asking her
what sex felt like.
She answered me with,
Do you ever touch yourself?
Sex is still a mystery,
with or without an answer.
The way the man in the subway
reads the paper
and folds it,
looks up for a second.
I've already concocted
a scenario.
He'd undress me.
I'd play with his cock.
I'd be on top
and I'd come
so hard that
it would reach my

tongue and I'd have to suck
on his ear to keep
my insides from spilling out.
My spent cunt—pleased and still now.

Red

She said *a country is always a woman.*
Why?
Blood and dirt in the wounds.
Do they ever heal?
No, but the borders change like our bellies.
See how the lines have switched
recently around the navel
how they swerve out
now that you've got a history.

*

Mother said when her father came to America
the only job he could find was cleaning toilets

in the Washington Heights Loews movie theater.
She saw *Gone with the Wind* for free.

When it was over he said in Schwäbisch,
"Don't you want to see it again?"

She said no, once was enough. She wanted
to go home, get on with becoming a citizen

paint her nails red.
She loved the fire escape

how it zee-d to the ground
reminding her of a way out.

The World's Fair

My cousin Dina tells me my father
took her to the 1940 New York World's fair.
She was 12 and Daddy was 22.
As she is speaking, I want so badly
to walk around the Flushing Meadows-Corona
park grounds, all 1,216 acres, with him,

to rewind time like on an old reel-to-reel,
hear the wheels whirring until that hot afternoon.
Her father had died several years before,
my father, a surrogate of sorts, wanted to show her
a good time, *to do something fun*, he told her,
away from Brooklyn.

"Dawn of a New Day" was its slogan.
I can imagine him
looking at the things of tomorrow,
pointing at the strange and unimaginable—
Air Conditioning, Wonder Bread, the Billy Rose Aquacade—
holding Dina's hand.

I remember his touch.
Once he had to give me a shot,
the needle went in and out
before I knew it
and he laughed when I said,
When will it hurt?

The Week of Missing Things and Prayers

The man with one arm tasted
grapes at the market, first red
then green.

> *Open my mouth and I will praise you*

All day I had that metallic
moon taste of 3 a.m.
sharp and lodged in the buds.

> *The Kaddish, the wide open sky, and my father*

On the subway a man with one eye
was chewing M&Ms—the schoolchildren looking
away, talking louder, pushing their bodies further out
as if the other eye was about us.

> *Plaques on the walls filled with names of the dead*
> *A constellation of what was*

There are moments in New York City that stop
the clock, its arms undone and set out
on the green with the hawk, her beauty
unfolding in the locked hour.

> *We open the ark and the Torah makes ten*
> *Hebrew alphabet light—lemon-lime salty*
> *I tasted their color*

Straw

The last time I saw my father
I brought him a glass of water
with a straw. He sipped with it
then winked at me the way he would,

with both eyes, his signature of approval.

That was last summer. The longing
comes over me from nowhere.
It hovers then snap—it bites
and I'm raw again.

Pelicans

We looked for shells
The pelicans diving in
        I thought of your posture

How straight you were
How you breathed in
        Your skin brown like almonds

I want to see you again.

You studied things
Behind the rope
        Rarely did you step over

The sun burns our feet
And the birds have surfaced
        As you do now.

Almost a Year Later

It's up in the leaves that I look for him.
The squirrels and robins busy,

Honeysuckle and white roses
Smelling of sex.

It's up in the green
That he lurks like some wild cat.

He'd say that the life of the mind is rich, my father,
And I'd think of the body.

The royal bones that hold us up.
Moonflowers wrap around

Bamboo and I'm waiting
For the white blossoms

The woman at the market promised.
She said it with conviction.

They'll open at night like the heart
And my hands and the whole race

On a hilltop in the distance—
Opening with a clarity.

After the Stroke

I bring her memoirs to read.
She likes them.
She tells me I lost my ass.
I reach back
and there it is

smaller, true, but still there.
I love my ass and tits.
Always have—thighs another matter,
now that I'm older
I'm liking them.

They've been there for me.
I feel her slipping away,
and as she slips, I feel
more inside me,
how strange this life

of her I've loved—
I never could let go.
Even now. It's her words that
have kept me distant,
with "you'll see when you get older,"

in this clear morning.
"We are all alone,"
she says. "Yes, mom,
we are all alone."
And then I close her orange door.

A dead raccoon lies
on Mosholu Parkway,
swollen and awful,
death, sweet death
amidst the fresh green leaves.

Each year—a tease
"See, it's new again
for you and only you,"
making me want even more, to be never complete,
but raw, dirt, her daughter.

I Find My Mother Here

In Brussels
        In its bread and cheese
                In the potatoes

In the light that keeps
        The old buildings standing
                It's here that I understand

Why she is who she is
        It's all hers
                Including me.

Hanukkah Haiku for My Dad

The light comes undone
Gray morning, leaves wet, mother
Alone without you.

Parts Suspended

Sweet death—
        lend me some wire,
wood and blue paint so that I can hover

with her tonight
        as you make your way
around my mother, her body

now angular as
        a Calder mobile
her clavicle;

a ship's mast, a lookout
        to that far-off country.
Panic sets in, she says,

in Rexingen the fields are the same.
        My father made mistakes.
We should have left earlier.

Two Weeks Before

Light birds of summer, their busy wings.
I make pictures with words
so that I can know you.

We're in July again
you, on the bed watching me
we have switched places—

a child now back in the Black Forest—
with your sister, mama and papa
like an accordion compressed

the Depends, Ensure—vanilla flavor,
the murmuring I can't make out.
You're ready, but I'm not.

I want to tell you more things.
Selfish in my wanting
even now. And you,

you want to fly through the grilles.
I want to say go, to let you go
the way we must, even with ourselves,

with our own flesh,
go sweet Mommy
fly with the birds of summer.

Storm King after Shiva

*

We sit in the *Gazebo for Two Anarchists*

Watch *Sea Change* and the *Easter Island Head* by Unknown

Bow to *Adonai* and the *Three Legged Buddha*

Eat chili at the café

Take the tram to the *Mermaid*.

How do you mark a life?

You go on.

There were woodchucks near *Mozart's Birthday*.

You were born on Beethoven's, December 16, 1923

Rexingen, Germany.

7 children
7 grandchildren
Big pots.

Mommy—rest now in the *Butterfly Chair* with me.

**

When you were alive
I saw your whole body
Your nipples weren't mine.

We are not the same person.

When you couldn't talk anymore you squeezed my hand.

Spheres up here in the North Woods

We go back to where we came from.

You would have liked *Five Open Squares Gyratory*

Suspended

XI Books III Apples.

The once farmland.

    ***

You said you were so happy when I was born.
You left the house with me in the carriage and a pink blanket.
We sat in the park—just you and me.

For My Parents

The cobblestones and rain
and you two
way before I was born—
I'm imagining you in Montmartre

>doing what newlyweds do
>with that light coming through
>naming what will become somehow
>your lives and mine, framed in this November afternoon.

I have this—dog shit on the sidewalk
the cluster of whores in the Pigalle
and loss thick through me—
both of you gone now.

>I'm spreading your words like ashes
>on the winding walk up to the view
>where they're selling trinkets.
>I'm setting you both free here

with the artists and beggars
and the blue pigeons that fan out
as if we are incidental
to the old bread strewn here and there.

Yizkor

The wild morning glories have
their moments of magnificence
and we often miss them.

      "It goes fast," my mother would say.
      Halloween candy appearing in supermarkets in August.
      Let me first live in the months of remembering.

The first Yom Kippur without my parents
I now recite two verses—
Teach me how to pray.

      After the fast, my father would come home
      from shul and my mother had
      eggs, herring and coffee waiting for him.

We'd eat. "It gets easier as you get older," he'd say.
It is easier now—the body knows,
how she didn't believe in God but in tradition, the geology of things—

      that you pass them on. The body knows
      and I know little as I sit in my chair.
      Teach me how to pray.

Part III

The Mannequin at Grand Central Station

This morning at the Pink Slip
she's dressed in a teal bra and panties—

her breasts—a statement of defiance
to gravity, aging, modesty.

In this economy, screw the whole world.
Yesterday she wore a purple thong—see-through.

I imagine she's what men want,
the men in liquor ads, drinks barely

visible—nautical themes, subliminal sex
ricocheting about like song birds.

That's what's been imprinted on the brain
since my birth in 1964, the last of seven,

my poor mother, I think as I nod
to my mannequin friend.

Across from her is Zaro's,
another display tempting us.

What would you choose—
a bustier or a baguette with butter?

Maybe an evening with both, one under each arm
as you commute with the human race.

The *Times*'s been running articles
on female arousal—guess what?

It's *non-specific* and *narcissistic*.
Let's pause for a moment.

Oh yes, much centers, too,
on *wanting to be wanted*.

Men don't look at me anymore.
In poetry they say

keep the line that turns you red and
x-out those you can't part with,

which brings us back to the Pink Slip.
She's poised just so

as if you could name her.
That's the thing about getting older.

Nobody names you—
a freedom worth earning on this side

of constellations we pass under
with tourists, the homeless, the National Guard,

all framed by bouquets in buckets
next to shoe shiners, loaves stacked

high, and her babydolls and teddies
already wrapped in tissue, waiting for someone else.

Turn Back the Clocks

Turn back the clocks at 2 a.m. when the moon
lounges on a soft bed of nothing,
pillows of light and shadow thrown about
like afterthoughts. See how she sits there.

No discussion necessary.
That's what the boss said the other day.
And what about freedom of expression?
Those three words we learned in elementary
school. Those words that stood there,
fields of wheat and corn in rows of desire
for what could be made—the opportunity.
Except no screaming *fire* in a theatre
when there is no fire. That's a crime.

So the crime here is not murder, my colleagues,
but dissent, a chestnut tree growing in a thousand directions.
My boss, let me tell you something you'll not hear.
A discussion is always necessary.

This game we have is as old as the moon.
Who wins?

*We the people of the United States, in order to form a more perfect union,
establish justice, insure domestic tranquility, provide for the common defense,
promote the general welfare, and secure the blessings of liberty to ourselves
and our posterity, do ordain and establish this Constitution for the United
States of America.*

Turn back the clocks. Sit down
in your classroom and listen to the teacher.
Listen as she talks.

*Congress shall make no law respecting an establishment of religion, or pro-
hibiting the free exercise thereof; or abridging the freedom of speech, or of
the press; or the right of the people peaceably to assemble, and to petition the
government for a redress of grievances.*

Were you moved by these declarations
or were you staring out the window
thinking of your next victim, even then?

Decorated Generals

Who said that scaffolding is temporary?
What happens if the work remains undone,
the center beams never come and all stands
askew indefinitely?

It's life, she said.
*Remember how the canoe
made the turtles scurry off the lily pads before you
could see them fully?*

Yes.
Well, that's how it is. You get glimpses of things.

*What you have now is an oar.
Move where you can and stay away from the big rocks.*

I want to be free from want
like before the snow came
and covered me in something
other than fire and ice.

Let want be.

It reminds me of the decorated generals—
how they want to make
peace at the end of their lives.
They come to the table
like children, hungry.

CV: On Looking for a Job

I'm a 47-year-old woman, mother of two, but you don't want to hear about that. It will not appear on my resume.

You want to hear that I can tweet, manage, market, write faster than lightning in crisp, fresh, grab-you-by-the-testicles language, and thrive in a collaborative, fast-paced environment. You want to note my greatest accomplishments, how I overcame obstacles at the workplace, how I compensate for my weaknesses, how I'd promote you, create buzz so you'd rise above the din, you nonprofit, holier-than-thou excuse for a place of employment.

Today you are such an enlightened synagogue; your rabbi is Episcopalian with a Hebrew name. Next week, you'll be one of the great institutions of higher education *that makes New York its playground*. Next month you'll be one of the formidable charities that will end global hunger and achieve world peace as soon as you hire that perfect candidate.

Stop looking at my breasts. No, keep looking at them it makes me feel young.

Ok—you mean you want me to come back three more times and repeat my wondrous feats in places of employment over the last 20 years and meet with your colleagues, who sit around a table and offer me beverages several times as if the conference room were the Sahara once the doors close, and who are both senior and junior to you, and who you really can't stand and would strangle if you were a tad more unstable.

After the third go around you'll tell me I don't have the job, perhaps by phone, or email, or better yet simply by form letter. Never mind that I've spent countless hours getting to know your place of employment (at this point I know your mission better than you do) and bought several suits on credit from Loehmann's so that you wouldn't have to see me in the same armor three times in a row. Never mind that I worked many hours on a strategic plan that you may use at some point to prove to your vice president of communications that you are thinking outside the box. In fact, after all is said and done, you'll tell me you decided to pick none of the finalists because none of them had the bright ideas you have no intention of ever implementing.

You—man in your fifties who should not be wearing suspenders—wish for a moment you were me, for the fleeting thrill that you could start over again instead of being stuck in the hell hole that I call a job, a ticket to health insurance, stability, college tuition, an answer at a party.

And tomorrow you'll be a younger woman, midpoint between my daughter's age and mine, who hasn't a clue about life—really—but no worries, I can pretend too. At which point I'll start to feel sorry for you, in spite of the fact that you won't offer me the position. You'll hire the one closer to your own age—the one that I passed in the waiting room—the one that looked like you with the bangs, heels, shiny bag, and the confidence that I should have by now.

Let us not forget to mention those online applications (the ones no human will ever see) that ask for the day, month, year, time, and weather of the day I graduated from middle school and whether I've ever committed a felony with ample space for explanations.

And let us pay homage to the human resources specialists, also known as human assets managers, who ask my desired salary range in hushed phone conversations and then tell me that a person-to-person meeting isn't necessary at this point in the process.

Finally, let us remember the secretary at one of the 501(c)'s in midtown who looks at me with compassion and actually has a hard-copy of my resume in her hand as she walks with me to the office of the person who will ask me about my work experiences and if I've ever encountered a crisis and how I dealt with it.

He may check out my ass, which will bring up all sorts of conflicting emotions. I will want him to be better looking.

His office will have a spider plant, water bottles, and a window. It will be raining that day, and his BlackBerry will be buzzing, in sync with the answers I will give while looking directly at him, after the secretary closes the door, and I take a seat and begin.

For a Woman Veteran

For your 8 years of service
12 medals
2 tours in Iraq.
For knowing that in your service
To our country you were raped
By our own.
"It looked like I really had my stuff together, but I was dying inside."
For what you called an overwhelming sense of awe and gratitude
after you left the shelter and moved into your own place.
For rage, for your rage.
For your daughter.
For your sketch of a pot of water boiling on a stove.

Making Do

It's the moon and mint
that will make you whole again.

She said it in July when darkness
Fell around us.

The airplanes flickering.
I thought I saw my father walking up

The street—his skin brown this time of year.
We'd talk for a few and he'd be on his way.

She said you have another name now.
    *

My mother made a salad from her garden,
I was watching her 86-year-old hands,

With her husband gone, she's making do
Or rising to the occasion,

As she says with her projects,
Her typewriter and her friends.

On 9/11 I called her and she said
If nothing is running walk home.
    *

They always come apart at the center
Right where you'd touch them if you could,

I'm surprised at the places of least resistance
They were the perfect henchmen, doing exactly

What was expected.
And I was fooled again.

But my middle is intact
Wild still.

Part IV

The Last Two

The last two tomatoes hang
on the vine still green.

They hold strong against
night rain and wind.

I'll bring them in soon
to ripen, but today

the sun is out—
red beginning on their bottoms,

frost somewhere out there—
far from my heart.

Summer Suits

In the suit department at Macy's I hear a woman say she is looking for the right thing to wear to the wake of her husband's friend who got killed in a motorcycle accident on the Taconic. She said it to a friend she met by chance in the petite section. Did you hear it on the news? No, the other said, I didn't and then added, I'm going to Lord & Taylor. There's nothing here. I pause and look up. She is right. There is nothing here. The woman who was looking said it too—there's nothing here.

Dark clouds are gathering about the Cross County Mall. The little girls running to their mommies excited by the huge lollipops, the imminent rain, everything whirling in that silver light that happens right before.

I want the day to matter, that's what I think as I get back into my car and remember how summer used to seem long. I have to plant tomatoes. Chives grow quickly with all the rain. Another season without daddy. We need to look right for the dead and the living.

Riding through Van Cortlandt Park in March

First yellow on willows
newborn color of choice
before the announcement of girl or boy.

I'm not sure who I am today—
neither flesh nor flower—
but thought engine.

The path is muddy,
my wheels make their way
through the public golf course.

Boys run past me, 2 x 2,
a kind of chariot,
I shift to the right.

March is the month
of not knowing,
hint of spring but not.

Mother said you could still get
a snow storm.
Father loved the month.

It was his month of guessing—
the math of it—
I can see him.

Where did they go?
I'm not the same.
Who are you?

I don't know.
I know that I love the not knowing.
I'm terrified by the trick in the road,

light feather drifting,
the way you look at me sometimes
and I want to hold you.

For Dora

Your blood in my veins.
D for Deborah my middle
name. We are still here.

Old Faithful

We wait for it to spew.
Sitting next to a woman who has come
here every summer since the 1960s,
she says the eruptions once lasted longer and soared higher,
making me think that things
seem that way when we
turn backwards.
I don't want to do that in Wyoming.
I want to believe
there never was a past.
Water shoots out,
the crowd oohs,
pointing and snapping photos.
We walk by neighboring
geysers—their pools blue, pink
purple, lemon-orange—along Firehole River
where kids run by its banks,
the sulfur steam rises and dogs bark.

Big Families

My brother married then had a baby.
I called and wished mazel tov.
He named him after my father's father who
dealt in textiles and knew the scriptures

backwards and forwards. I found these things out
from my other brother. That was last year.
This is how families run like streams
from the mountain top, out to sea.

Leaving the Garden

Before the apple, Adam and Eve
Lounged around in nothing, not a blush.

The same with my children.
I wash their bodies.

There's nothing extra
maybe some scars on the knees,

from pavement falls, but they are
what they should be.

When they run through the gates
where will I be?

Jasper Summer

I hide in Indian paintbrush
        heather and anemone.

Rock and blue
        Light and green.

It starts snowing.
        Marmots look for cover.

The lake reflects glaciers—all is double
        form then water.

I only know
        Which is true

When our hipbones touch
        And you say

That light lives as long
        As you let it—silt filling us

Horn, tail, fin—
        With things other than ourselves.

Into the Moonlight

When you walk out
      I wait for your footsteps.

When you walk out
      I see your shadow.

When you walk out
      I hear the owl call.

When you walk out
      I lock the door.

August

Boats shimmy on the river.
Bikers and skateboarders fly by
without helmets as though they are invincible.
They are tonight
for we are all floating
in the summers of ourselves.
The 20-somethings hover about,
loud but soothing, too,
like crickets rubbing their parts together,
a city transfixed.
Further down, the couple on the long pier
kiss in that way that makes you
remember when he pulled you tight.
It was new, and now you wish that you had a chance
to do it all over somehow—
like the boats—how they roll
from side to side yet stay put.
This night is lit with a full moon,
it hangs over the ghastly Trump towers—
You reach up and touch it.

Part V

Here

She tells me I have to be patient.
I ask for how long.

A long time.
Tell me what I'm waiting for.

You're waiting for the moment when you stop worrying.
About what?

About everything.
Even about the man from India who says my computer will be ok?

Yes.
I want to know when I'll stop missing my parents.

Never—they'll be in the distance—always.
How about new loves?

They'll come and go—some will stay forever.
And how will that be?

Terrible and lovely in unequal parts.
How can that be?

They'll be no end and no beginning.
Just a wide open middle—a sea?

Yes—a middle that will be unbearably beautiful.
Then what?

You have to decide.
What do I do?

You'll know—your body will tell you.
My body tells me pleasure.

Then pleasure it until there's nothing left.
I'm almost there.

Good—keep at it.
The sun's coming up.

Lick it.
It tastes like 16.

Taste 46—
Scattered.

Tell me more.
I can't—I want everything.

You mean you want to make love to the world.
Yes—rocking chair.

Tell me more.
I can't—just that I love.

Who?
They know.

Say it more than once.
Why?

Because you're here.
Where?

Here.

The Fish

She disappears below the surface
of the river for what seems like a long time
and then appears with a fish,

her profile distorted
against the turning leaves.
We also dive where it's murky.

I struggle to rearrange.
It's where you find
what you weren't looking for.

Just yesterday I found
my first love notes
and Daddy, too.

He was saying something about the bread—
how it rose all night.
We'd better put it in the oven.

But I don't come up
with a fish in my mouth,
no, just the light

coming off the bridge,
and the woman next to me
who's fallen asleep in her seat.

Graffiti

The light seeps in

        She says *that's what spring is for*

Don't reach so much

Stay still

How?
It's hard in New York

Yes

        Graffiti bubble word: *Mercy*

Flickers like fire

Take note

The Violin

I want the music to run
through me like words
how they enter
as if they were living things,
a mosquito pushing its stinger in
slap it, blood.

The textbook had diagrams
the atria, ventricles and vena cava—superior and inferior—
we'd have to memorize the flow,
the process of cleansing and revelation,
to name the parts,

but I wanted to label firsts.
Here's where love sat, right here, reckless night parade.
Oh and here's where the bullet went in,
an empty shell sits there
you can put your ear to it
and hear him still.

Here's jealousy, prickly porcupine.
There's lust—it takes over,
a night owl. Loins fiery—cream and sugar please.
Then death, see Daddy,
see the hole raw—still.
His body a boat now.

New love, see it there
at the corner.
Take me home, make me whole.
See how she plays the violin:
do it that way, but say nothing.

On This Mountain

Wind from the east
shifts the air and your hair
making its own geometry.

Below us the black bear
watches her young
go off for good.

The hawks fly
over us
like bright ideas.

Two Lives

She said she had another life
somewhere between here
and the lighthouse.

How do you have two lives?
She said one is of the mind
the other of flesh.

Where's the life of the mind?
That's the one you can touch
but never hold—like water and regret.

It could have been but isn't.
The life of the flesh
has peppermint leaves.

Where do they meet?
On the corner in some town where
the flowerboxes are so close

to the street you can run
your hands over them.
What happens then?

Nothing—they eye each other
with suspicion and move on
like strays and the sea.

She said she had another life
somewhere between here
and the lighthouse.

Big Basket of Want

She said, *you can't expect that people will know.*
I said, know what?

That you are in need.
Of what?

All the things that you talk about to yourself when you are alone.
True, I tell them to the naked trees.

She said, *I know you do. I hear you.*
Oh, I'll speak softer next time.

No, you've got to tell the world.
What?

That you are a big basket of want.
What do I want?

You want people to love you so much that your insides come undone.
Then what?

You'll pick up the pieces, put them back, have a cherry border.
Will I let them cross it?

Sometimes—it will be up to you.

Baruch Habah

Baruch Habah, blessed who comes
into my life and makes it whole—
the night of fruit
the day of forever
wanting to be blessed
with a new direction
a new song,
an apple at dawn—
Where did you come from?

Prayer

I plant Armenian cucumbers,
Chinese lanterns and peas.

The rain all day for days
makes the soil dark and rich

with something more. When I push my
finger through and pour seeds

it is a prayer for something better.
The robins with their porn-orange breasts

poke for worms.
I want to be a robin on a mission.

On my walk, a garter snake
hides under a log.

I keep hearing her on
my way back—

strange and melodious.
She tells me every season

has moments of grace
and that it is my job

to find them.
Ah and how? I ask.

That's when there is silence again.
She uses big words for a snake.

Notes

"Storm King after Shiva" refers to the Storm King Art Center, located in New Windsor, New York. With over 500 acres of fields and woodlands, Storm King provides an outdoor setting for more than 100 sculptures, some of which are enormous. In Judaism, shiva is the week-long mourning period after burial.

"Yizkor" refers to a Jewish service for commemorating the dead.

"For a Woman Veteran" was inspired by the February 27, 2013 *New York Times* article, "Trauma Sets Female Veterans Adrift Back Home," by Patricia Leigh Brown.

"For Dora" refers to Dora Schweitzer, my great-grandmother, who was killed in the Theresienstadt concentration camp.

www.ingramcontent.com/pod-product-compliance
Lightning Source LLC
Chambersburg PA
CBHW070058100426
42743CB00012B/2585